Gospel
G/C diatonic accordion
Solos

Ondřej Šárek

Contents

Introduction	3
How to read tablature	3
Button layouts	4
Songs	
Amazing Grace	5,6
Angel Band	7,8
The Angel Rolled the Stone Away	9,10
Are You Washed in the Blood	11, 12
Crying Holy	13, 14
Father Abraham	15
Gimme Dat Ol'Time Religion	16, 17
Go down Moses	18, 19
Go, Tell It on the Mountains	20, 21
Heav'n	22, 23
I'm A Pilgrim	24, 25
I'm Gonna Sing	26
Joshua Fit the Battle of Jericho	27, 28
Kum Ba Yah	29, 30
Mary had a baby	31
Michael, Row the boat Ashore	32
Nobody Knows the Trouble I've Seen	33, 34
Oh Freedom	35
Oh, Sinner man	36
Oh, When the Saints	37, 38
Rock My Soul	39
Singin' With a Sword in My Hand	40, 41
Standing in the Need of Prayer	42, 43
Steal Away	44, 45
Swing Low, Sweet Chariot	46, 47
Wayfaring Stranger	48, 49
Were You There When They Crucified My Lord?	50, 51

Introduction

acred music is often played. But there is a problem when the player wants to play a solo on an G/C diatonic
ccordion.
or the reason the book was written. You can find here 27 gospels and spirituals. Each song is arranged in two
ales.
nd now you can start playing, singing and worshiping our Lord.

How to read tablature

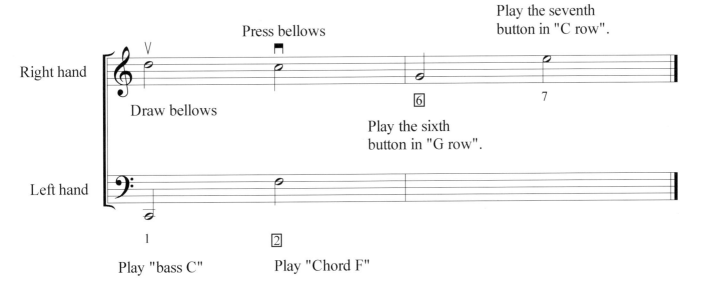

Button Layouts G/C

Score

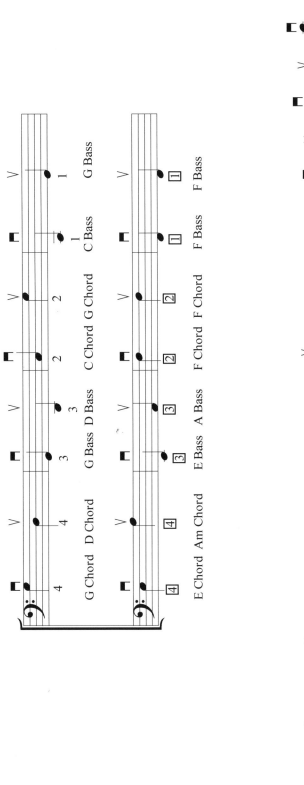

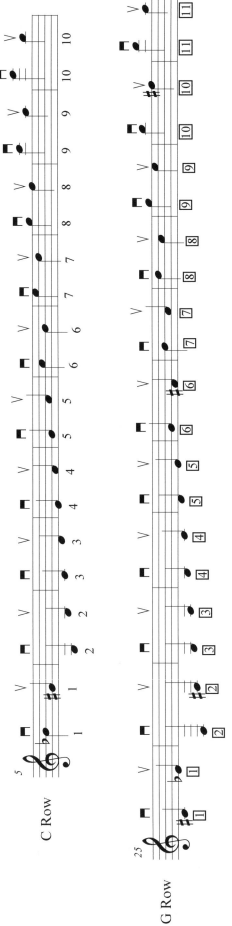

Amazing Grace

arr: Ondřej Šárek

Amazing Grace

arr: Ondřej Šárek

Angel Band

arr: Ondřej Šárek

Angel Band

arr: Ondřej Šárek

The Angel Rolled The Stone Away

arr: Ondřej Šárek

The Angel Rolled The Stone Away

arr: Ondřej Šárek

Are You Washed in the Blood

arr: Ondřej Šárek

Are You Washed in the Blood

arr: Ondřej Šárek

Crying Holy

arr: Ondřej Šárek

Crying Holy

arr: Ondřej Šárek

Father Abraham

arr: Ondřej Šárek

Father Abraham

arr: Ondřej Šárek

Gimme Dat Ol'Time Religion

arr: Ondřej Šárek

Gimme Dat Ol'Time Religion

arr: Ondřej Šárek

Go Down Moses

arr: Ondřej Šárek

Go Down Moses

arr: Ondřej Šárek

Go, Tell It On The Mountains

arr: Ondřej Šárek

Go, Tell It On The Mountains

arr: Ondřej Šárek

Heav'n

arr: Ondřej Šárek

Heav'n

arr: Ondřej Šárek

I'm A Pilgrim

arr: Ondřej Šárek

I'm A Pilgrim

arr: Ondřej Šárek

I'm Gonna Sing

arr: Ondřej Šárek

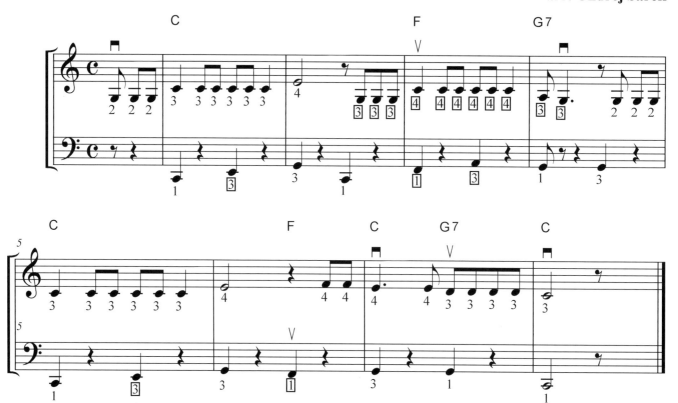

I'm Gonna Sing

arr: Ondřej Šárek

Joshua Fit the Battle of Jericho

arr: Ondřej Šárek

Joshua Fit the Battle of Jericho

arr: Ondřej Šárek

Kum ba yah

arr: Ondřej Šárek

Kum ba yah

arr: Ondřej Šárek

Mary Had A Baby

Arr: Ondřej Šárek

Mary Had A Baby

Arr: Ondřej Šárek

Michael, Row The boat Ashore

arr: Ondřej Šárek

Michael, Row The boat Ashore

arr: Ondřej Šárek

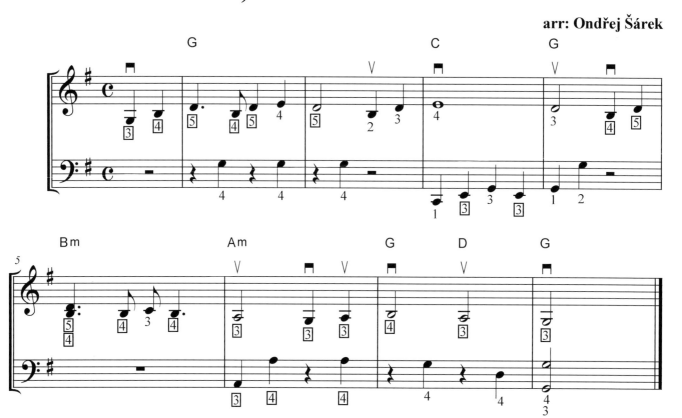

Nobody Knows The Trouble I've Seen

arr: Ondřej Šárek

Nobody Knows The Trouble I've Seen

arr: Ondřej Šárek

Oh Freedom

arr: Ondřej Šárek

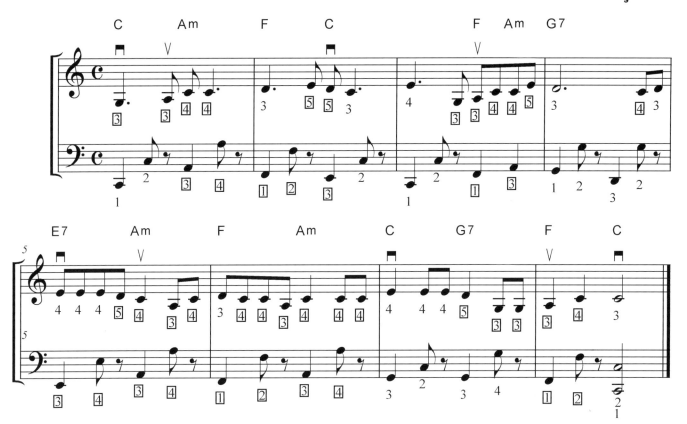

Oh Freedom

arr: Ondřej Šárek

Oh, Sinner man

Am   G   arr: Ondřej Šárek

Oh, Sinner man

Em   D   arr: Ondřej Šárek

Oh, When The Saints

arr: Ondřej Šárek

Oh, When The Saints

arr: Ondřej Šárek

Rock My Soul

arr: Ondřej Šárek

Rock My Soul

arr: Ondřej Šárek

Singin' With A Sword In My Hand

arr: Ondřej Šárek

Singin' With A Sword In My Hand

arr: Ondřej Šárek

Copyright © 2013 Ondřej Šárek

Standing in the Need of Prayer

arr: Ondřej Šárek

Standing in the Need of Prayer

arr: Ondřej Šárek

Steal Away

arr: Ondřej Šárek

Steal Away

arr: Ondřej Šárek

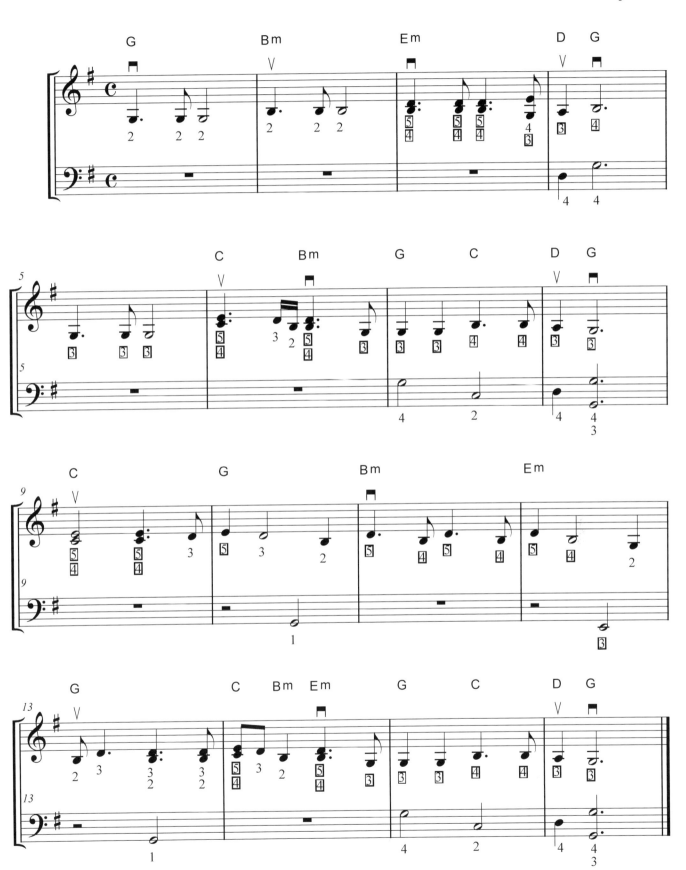

Swing Low, Sweet Chariot

arr: Ondřej Šárek

Swing Low, Sweet Chariot

arr: Ondřej Šárek

Wayfaring Stranger

arr: Ondřej Šárek

Wayfaring Stranger

arr: Ondřej Šárek

Were You There When They Crucified My Lord?

arr: Ondřej Šárek

Were You There When They Crucified My Lord?

arr: Ondřej Šárek

New Anglo Concertina books

For C/G 30-button Wheatstone Lachenal System
Gospel Anglo Concertina Solos (CreateSpace Independent Publishing Platform)
Notebook for Anna Magdalena Bach and Anglo Concertina (CreateSpace Independent Publishing Platform)
Robert Burns songs for Anglo Concertina (CreateSpace Independent Publishing Platform)

Coming soon!
The Czech Lute for Anglo Concertina (CreateSpace Independent Publishing Platform)
Gregorian chant for Anglo Concertina (CreateSpace Independent Publishing Platform)

For C/G 20-button
Gospel C/G Anglo Concertina Solos (CreateSpace Independent Publishing Platform)
Robert Burns songs for C/G Anglo Concertina (CreateSpace Independent Publishing Platform)

Coming soon!
Gregorian chant for C/G Anglo Concertina (CreateSpace Independent Publishing Platform)

New Diatonic Accordion (Melodeon) books

For G/C diatonic accordion
Bass songbook for G/C melodeon (CreateSpace Independent Publishing Platform)
Cross row style songbook for beginner G/C diatonic accordion (CreateSpace Independent Publishing Platform)
Gospel G/C diatonic accordion Solos (CreateSpace Independent Publishing Platform)

For C/F diatonic accordion
Cross row style songbook for beginner C/F diatonic accordion (CreateSpace Independent Publishing Platform)
Gospel C/F diatonic accordion Solos (CreateSpace Independent Publishing Platform)

For D/G diatonic accordion
Cross row style songbook for beginner D/G diatonic accordion (CreateSpace Independent Publishing Platform)
Gospel D/G diatonic accordion Solos (CreateSpace Independent Publishing Platform)

Ukulele Duets

Notebook for Anna Magdalena Bach, C tuning ukulele and C tuning ukulele (CreateSpace Independent Publishing Platform)
Notebook for Anna Magdalena Bach, C tuning ukulele and Ukulele with low G (CreateSpace Independent Publishing Platform)
Notebook for Anna Magdalena Bach, C tuning ukulele and Baritone ukulele (CreateSpace Independent Publishing Platform)
Notebook for Anna Magdalena Bach, Ukulele with low G and Ukulele with low G (CreateSpace Independent Publishing Platform)
Notebook for Anna Magdalena Bach, Ukulele with low G and Baritone ukulele (CreateSpace Independent Publishing Platform)
Notebook for Anna Magdalena Bach, Baritone ukulele and Baritone ukulele (CreateSpace Independent Publishing Platform)

New Ukulele books

For C tuning ukulele

Classics for Ukulele (Mel Bay Publications)
Ukulele Bluegrass Solos (Mel Bay Publications)
Antonin Dvorak: Biblical Songs (CreateSpace Independent Publishing Platform)
Irish tunes for all ukulele (CreateSpace Independent Publishing Platform)
Gospel Ukulele Solos (CreateSpace Independent Publishing Platform)
Gregorian chant for Ukulele (CreateSpace Independent Publishing Platform)
The Czech Lute for Ukulele (CreateSpace Independent Publishing Platform)
Romantic Pieces by Frantisek Max Knize for Ukulele (CreateSpace Independent Publishing Platform)
Notebook for Anna Magdalena Bach and Ukulele (CreateSpace Independent Publishing Platform)
Open Tunings for Ukulel (Mel Bay Publications)
Robert Burns songs for ukulele (CreateSpace Independent Publishing Platform)
Jewish songs for C tuning ukulele (CreateSpace Independent Publishing Platform)
Campanella style songbook for beginner: C tuning ukulele (CreateSpace Independent Publishing Platform)

For C tuning with low G

Irish tunes for all ukulele (CreateSpace Independent Publishing Platform)
Gospel Ukulele low G Solos (CreateSpace Independent Publishing Platform)
Antonin Dvorak: Biblical Songs: for Ukulele with low G (CreateSpace Independent Publishing Platform)
Gregorian chant for Ukulele with low G (CreateSpace Independent Publishing Platform)
The Czech Lute for Ukulele with low G (CreateSpace Independent Publishing Platform)
Romantic Pieces by Frantisek Max Knize for Ukulele with low G (CreateSpace Independent Publishing Platform)
Notebook for Anna Magdalena Bach and Ukulele with low G (CreateSpace Independent Publishing Platform)
Robert Burns songs for ukulele with low G (CreateSpace Independent Publishing Platform)
Jewish songs for ukulele with low G (CreateSpace Independent Publishing Platform)
Campanella style songbook for beginner: ukulele with low G (CreateSpace Independent Publishing Platform)

For Baritone ukulele

Irish tunes for all ukulele (CreateSpace Independent Publishing Platform)
Gospel Baritone Ukulele Solos (CreateSpace Independent Publishing Platform)

Antonin Dvorak: Biblical Songs: for Baritone Ukulele (CreateSpace Independent Publishing Platform)

Gregorian chant for Baritone Ukulele (CreateSpace Independent Publishing Platform)
The Czech Lute for Baritone Ukulele (CreateSpace Independent Publishing Platform)
Romantic Pieces by Frantisek Max Knize for Baritone Ukulele (CreateSpace Independent Publishing Platform)
Notebook for Anna Magdalena Bach and Baritone Ukulele (CreateSpace Independent Publishing Platform)
Robert Burns songs for Baritone ukulele (CreateSpace Independent Publishing Platform)
Jewish songs for baritone ukulele (CreateSpace Independent Publishing Platform)
Campanella style songbook for beginner: Baritone ukulele (CreateSpace Independent Publishing Platform)

For Baritone ukulele with high D

Jewish songs for baritone ukulele with high D (CreateSpace Independent Publishing Platform)
Campanella style songbook for beginner: Baritone ukulele with high D (CreateSpace Independent Publishing Platform)

For 6 sting ukulele (Lili'u ukulele)

Gospel 6 string Ukulele Solos (CreateSpace Independent Publishing Platform)
Gregorian chant for 6 string Ukulele (CreateSpace Independent Publishing Platform)
Notebook for Anna Magdalena Bach and 6 string Ukulele (CreateSpace Independent Publishing Platform)
Robert Burns songs for 6 string ukulele (CreateSpace Independent Publishing Platform)

For Slide ukulele (lap steel ukulele)

Comprehensive Slide Ukulele: Guidance for Slide Ukulele Playing (CreateSpace Independent Publishing Platform)
Gospel Slide Ukulele Solos (CreateSpace Independent Publishing Platform)
Irish tunes for slide ukulele (CreateSpace Independent Publishing Platform)
Robert Burns songs for Slide ukulele (CreateSpace Independent Publishing Platform)

For D tuning ukulele

Skola hry na ukulele (G+W s.r.o.)
Irish tunes for all ukulele (CreateSpace Independent Publishing Platform)
Jewish songs for D tuning ukulele (CreateSpace Independent Publishing Platform)
Campanella style songbook for beginner: D tuning ukulele (CreateSpace Independent Publishing Platform)

Made in the USA
Middletown, DE
15 May 2022